CORNHUSKERS

BY

CARL SANDBURG

NEW YORK

HENRY HOLT AND COMPANY

1918

THE QUINN & BODEN CO. PRESS
RAHWAY, N. J.

TO

JANET AND MARGARET

Acknowledgement is set forth that some things here were first printed in Poetry: A Magazine of Verse, The Chicago Daily News, and the service of the Newspaper Enterprise Association.—C. S.

CONTENTS

LEATHER LEGGINGS

Contents

CORNHUSKERS

PRAIRIE

I WAS born on the prairie and the milk of its wheat, the
red of its clover, the eyes of its women, gave me
a song and a slogan.

Here the water went down, the icebergs slid with gravel,
the gaps and the valleys hissed, and the black loam
came, and the yellow sandy loam.

Here between the sheds of the Rocky Mountains and the
Appalachians, here now a morning star fixes a fire
sign over the timber claims and cow pastures, the
corn belt, the cotton belt, the cattle ranches.

Here the gray geese go five hundred miles and back
with a wind under their wings honking the cry for
a new home.

Here I know I will hanker after nothing so much as
one more sunrise or a sky moon of fire doubled
to a river moon of water.

The prairie sings to me in the forenoon and I know in
the night I rest easy in the prairie arms, on the
prairie heart.

. . .

              After the sunburn of the day
              handling a pitchfork at a hayrack,
              after the eggs and biscuit and coffee,
              the pearl-gray haystacks
              in the gloaming
              are cool prayers
              to the harvest hands.

In the city among the walls the overland passenger train
    is choked and the pistons hiss and the wheels curse.
On the prairie the overland flits on phantom wheels and
    the sky and the soil between them muffle the pistons
    and cheer the wheels.

        .   .   .

I am here when the cities are gone.
I am here before the cities come.
I nourished the lonely men on horses.
I will keep the laughing men who ride iron.
I am dust of men.

The running water babbled to the deer, the cottontail,
    the gopher.
You came in wagons, making streets and schools,
Kin of the ax and rifle, kin of the plow and horse,
Singing *Yankee Doodle, Old Dan Tucker, Turkey in the
    Straw,*
You in the coonskin cap at a log house door hearing a
    lone wolf howl,
You at a sod house door reading the blizzards and
    chinooks let loose from Medicine Hat,
I am dust of your dust, as I am brother and mother
To the copper faces, the worker in flint and clay,
The singing women and their sons a thousand years
    ago
Marching single file the timber and the plain.

I hold the dust of these amid changing stars.
I last while old wars are fought, while peace broods
    mother-like,
While new wars arise and the fresh killings of young
    men.

I fed the boys who went to France in great dark days.
Appomattox is a beautiful word to me and so is Valley
    Forge and the Marne and Verdun,
I who have seen the red births and the red deaths
Of sons and daughters, I take peace or war, I say
    nothing and wait.

Have you seen a red sunset drip over one of my corn-
    fields, the shore of night stars, the wave lines of
    dawn up a wheat valley?
Have you heard my threshing crews yelling in the chaff
    of a strawpile and the running wheat of the wagon-
    boards, my cornhuskers, my harvest hands hauling
    crops, singing dreams of women, worlds, horizons?

                    .   .   .

            Rivers cut a path on flat lands.
            The mountains stand up.
            The salt oceans press in
            And push on the coast lines.
            The sun, the wind, bring rain
            And I know what the rainbow writes across
                the east or west in a half-circle:
            A love-letter pledge to come again.

                    .   .   .

            Towns on the Soo Line,
            Towns on the Big Muddy,
            Laugh at each other for cubs
            And tease as children.

Omaha and Kansas City, Minneapolis and St. Paul,
    sisters in a house together, throwing slang, growing
    up.
Towns in the Ozarks, Dakota wheat towns, Wichita,
    Peoria, Buffalo, sisters throwing slang, growing up.

                    .   .   .

Out of prairie-brown grass crossed with a streamer of
    wigwam smoke—out of a smoke pillar, a blue
    promise—out of wild ducks woven in greens and
    purples—
Here I saw a city rise and say to the peoples round
    world: Listen, I am strong, I know what I want.
Out of log houses and stumps—canoes stripped from
    tree-sides—flatboats coaxed with an ax from the
    timber claims—in the years when the red and the
    white men met—the houses and streets rose.

A thousand red men cried and went away to new places
    for corn and women: a million white men came and
    put up skyscrapers, threw out rails and wires, feelers
    to the salt sea: now the smokestacks bite the skyline
    with stub teeth.

In an early year the call of a wild duck woven in greens
    and purples: now the riveter's chatter, the police
    patrol, the song-whistle of the steamboat.

To a man across a thousand years I offer a handshake.
I say to him: Brother, make the story short, for the
    stretch of a thousand years is short.

        . . .

What brothers these in the dark?
What eaves of skyscrapers against a smoke moon?
These chimneys shaking on the lumber shanties
When the coal boats plow by on the river—
The hunched shoulders of the grain elevators—
The flame sprockets of the sheet steel mills
And the men in the rolling mills with their shirts off

Playing their flesh arms against the twisting wrists of
    steel:
        what brothers these
        in the dark
        of a thousand years?

. . .

A headlight searches a snowstorm.
A funnel of white light shoots from over the pilot of
    the Pioneer Limited crossing Wisconsin.

In the morning hours, in the dawn,
The sun puts out the stars of the sky
And the headlight of the Limited train.

The fireman waves his hand to a country school teacher
    on a bobsled.
A boy, yellow hair, red scarf and mittens, on the bob-
    sled, in his lunch box a pork chop sandwich and a
    V of gooseberry pie.

The horses fathom a snow to their knees.
Snow hats are on the rolling prairie hills.
The Mississippi bluffs wear snow hats.

. . .

Keep your hogs on changing corn and mashes of grain,
    O farmerman.
    Cram their insides till they waddle on short legs
    Under the drums of bellies, hams of fat.
    Kill your hogs with a knife slit under the ear.
    Hack them with cleavers.
    Hang them with hooks in the hind legs.

. . .

A wagonload of radishes on a summer morning.

Sprinkles of dew on the crimson-purple balls.

The farmer on the seat dangles the reins on the rumps
of dapple-gray horses.

The farmer's daughter with a basket of eggs dreams of
a new hat to wear to the county fair.

. . .

On the left- and right-hand side of the road,
Marching corn—

I saw it knee high weeks ago—now it is head high—
tassels of red silk creep at the ends of the ears.

. . .

I am the prairie, mother of men, waiting.

They are mine, the threshing crews eating beefsteak, the
farmboys driving steers to the railroad cattle pens.

They are mine, the crowds of people at a Fourth of July
basket picnic, listening to a lawyer read the Declara-
tion of Independence, watching the pinwheels and
Roman candles at night, the young men and women
two by two hunting the bypaths and kissing bridges.

They are mine, the horses looking over a fence in the
frost of late October saying good-morning to the
horses hauling wagons of rutabaga to market.

They are mine, the old zigzag rail fences, the new barb
wire.   . . .

The cornhuskers wear leather on their hands.

There is no let-up to the wind.

Blue bandannas are knotted at the ruddy chins.

Falltime and winter apples take on the smolder of the
five-o'clock November sunset: falltime, leaves, bon-
fires, stubble, the old things go, and the earth is
grizzled.

The land and the people hold memories, even among the
anthills and the angleworms, among the toads and
woodroaches—among gravestone writings rubbed
out by the rain—they keep old things that never
grow old.

The frost loosens corn husks.
The sun, the rain, the wind
            loosen corn husks.
The men and women are helpers.
They are all cornhuskers together.
I see them late in the western evening
            in a smoke-red dust.

            .   .   .

The phantom of a yellow rooster flaunting a scarlet
comb, on top of a dung pile crying hallelujah to
the streaks of daylight,
The phantom of an old hunting dog nosing in the underbrush for muskrats, barking at a coon in a treetop
at midnight, chewing a bone, chasing his tail round
a corncrib,
The phantom of an old workhorse taking the steel point
of a plow across a forty-acre field in spring, hitched
to a harrow in summer, hitched to a wagon among
cornshocks in fall,
These phantoms come into the talk and wonder of
people on the front porch of a farmhouse late
summer nights.
" The shapes that are gone are here," said an old man
with a cob pipe in his teeth one night in Kansas
with a hot wind on the alfalfa.

            .   .   .

Look at six eggs
In a mockingbird's nest.

Listen to six mockingbirds
Flinging follies of O-be-joyful
Over the marshes and uplands.

Look at songs
Hidden in eggs.

. . .

When the morning sun is on the trumpet-vine blossoms,
sing at the kitchen pans: Shout All Over God's
Heaven.

When the rain slants on the potato hills and the sun
plays a silver shaft on the last shower, sing to the
bush at the backyard fence: Mighty Lak a Rose.

When the icy sleet pounds on the storm windows and
the house lifts to a great breath, sing for the out-
side hills: The Ole Sheep Done Know the Road,
the Young Lambs Must Find the Way.

. . .

Spring slips back with a girl face calling always: " Any
new songs for me? Any new songs? "

O prairie girl, be lonely, singing, dreaming, waiting—
your lover comes—your child comes—the years
creep with toes of April rain on new-turned sod.

O prairie girl, whoever leaves you only crimson poppies
to talk with, whoever puts a good-by kiss on your
lips and never comes back—

There is a song deep as the falltime redhaws, long as
the layer of black loam we go to, the shine of the
morning star over the corn belt, the wave line of
dawn up a wheat valley.

. . .

O prairie mother, I am one of your boys.

I have loved the prairie as a man with a heart shot
full of pain over love.

Here I know I will hanker after nothing so much as
one more sunrise or a sky moon of fire doubled to
a river moon of water.

. . .

I speak of new cities and new people.

I tell you the past is a bucket of ashes.

I tell you yesterday is a wind gone down,
a sun dropped in the west.

I tell you there is nothing in the world
only an ocean of to-morrows,
a sky of to-morrows.

I am a brother of the cornhuskers who say
at sundown:
To-morrow is a day.

RIVER ROADS

LET the crows go by hawking their caw and caw.
They have been swimming in midnights of coal mines
somewhere.
Let 'em hawk their caw and caw.

Let the woodpecker drum and drum on a hickory stump.
He has been swimming in red and blue pools somewhere
hundreds of years
And the blue has gone to his wings and the red has
gone to his head.
Let his red head drum and drum.

Let the dark pools hold the birds in a looking-glass.
And if the pool wishes, let it shiver to the blur of many
wings, old swimmers from old places.

Let the redwing streak a line of vermillion on the green
wood lines.
And the mist along the river fix its purple in lines of
a woman's shawl on lazy shoulders.

PRAIRIE WATERS BY NIGHT

CHATTER of birds two by two raises a night song joining
a litany of running water—sheer waters showing the
russet of old stones remembering many rains.

And the long willows drowse on the shoulders of the
running water, and sleep from much music; joined
songs of day-end, feathery throats and stony waters,
in a choir chanting new psalms.

It is too much for the long willows when low laughter
of a red moon comes down; and the willows drowse
and sleep on the shoulders of the running water.

EARLY MOON

THE baby moon, a canoe, a silver papoose canoe, sails and sails in the Indian west.

A ring of silver foxes, a mist of silver foxes, sit and sit around the Indian moon.

One yellow star for a runner, and rows of blue stars for more runners, keep a line of watchers.

O foxes, baby moon, runners, you are the panel of memory, fire-white writing to-night of the Red Man's dreams.

Who squats, legs crossed and arms folded, matching its look against the moon-face, the star-faces, of the West?

Who are the Mississippi Valley ghosts, of copper foreheads, riding wiry ponies in the night?—no bridles, love-arms on the pony necks, riding in the night a long old trail?

Why do they always come back when the silver foxes sit around the early moon, a silver papoose, in the Indian west?

LAUGHING CORN

THERE was a high majestic fooling
Day before yesterday in the yellow corn.

And day after to-morrow in the yellow corn
There will be high majestic fooling.

The ears ripen in late summer
And come on with a conquering laughter,
Come on with a high and conquering laughter.

The long-tailed blackbirds are hoarse.
One of the smaller blackbirds chitters on a stalk
And a spot of red is on its shoulder
And I never heard its name in my life.

Some of the ears are bursting.
A white juice works inside.
Cornsilk creeps in the end and dangles in the wind.
Always—I never knew it any other way—
The wind and the corn talk things over together.
And the rain and the corn and the sun and the corn
Talk things over together.

Over the road is the farmhouse.
The siding is white and a green blind is slung loose.
It will not be fixed till the corn is husked.
The farmer and his wife talk things over together.

AUTUMN MOVEMENT

I CRIED over beautiful things knowing no beautiful thing
lasts.

The field of cornflower yellow is a scarf at the neck of
the copper sunburned woman, the mother of the
year, the taker of seeds.

The northwest wind comes and the yellow is torn full
of holes, new beautiful things come in the first spit
of snow on the northwest wind, and the old things
go, not one lasts.

FALLTIME

GOLD of a ripe oat straw, gold of a southwest moon,
Canada thistle blue and flimmering larkspur blue,
Tomatoes shining in the October sun with red hearts,
Shining five and six in a row on a wooden fence,
Why do you keep wishes on your faces all day long,
Wishes like women with half-forgotten lovers going to
    new cities?
What is there for you in the birds, the birds, the birds,
    crying down on the north wind in September, acres
    of birds spotting the air going south?
Is there something finished? And some new beginning
    on the way?

ILLINOIS FARMER

Bury this old Illinois farmer with respect.
He slept the Illinois nights of his life after days of work
    in Illinois cornfields.
Now he goes on a long sleep.
The wind he listened to in the cornsilk and the tassels,
    the wind that combed his red beard zero mornings
    when the snow lay white on the yellow ears in the
    bushel basket at the corncrib,
The same wind will now blow over the place here where
    his hands must dream of Illinois corn.

HITS AND RUNS

I REMEMBER the Chillicothe ball players grappling the
Rock Island ball players in a sixteen-inning game
ended by darkness.
And the shoulders of the Chillicothe players were a red
smoke against the sundown and the shoulders of
the Rock Island players were a yellow smoke against
the sundown.
And the umpire's voice was hoarse calling balls and
strikes and outs and the umpire's throat fought in
the dust for a song.

VILLAGE IN LATE SUMMER

Lips half-willing in a doorway.
Lips half-singing at a window.
Eyes half-dreaming in the walls.
Feet half-dancing in a kitchen.
Even the clocks half-yawn the hours
And the farmers make half-answers.

BLIZZARD NOTES

I DON'T blame the kettle drums—they are hungry.
And the snare drums—I know what they want—they
are empty too.
And the harring booming bass drums—they are hungriest
of all.

      . . .

The howling spears of the Northwest die down.
The lullabies of the Southwest get a chance, a mother
song.
A cradle moon rides out of a torn hole in the ragbag
top of the sky.

SUNSET FROM OMAHA HOTEL WINDOW

Into the blue river hills
The red sun runners go
And the long sand changes
And to-day is a goner
And to-day is not worth haggling over.

Here in Omaha
The gloaming is bitter
As in Chicago
Or Kenosha.

The long sand changes.
To-day is a goner.
Time knocks in another brass nail.
Another yellow plunger shoots the dark.

Constellations
Wheeling over Omaha
As in Chicago
Or Kenosha.

The long sand is gone
and all the talk is stars.
They circle in a dome over Nebraska.

STILL LIFE

Cool your heels on the rail of an observation car.
Let the engineer open her up for ninety miles an hour.
Take in the prairie right and left, rolling land and new
    hay crops, swaths of new hay laid in the sun.
A gray village flecks by and the horses hitched in front
    of the post-office never blink an eye.
A barnyard and fifteen Holstein cows, dabs of white on
    a black wall map, never blink an eye.
A signalman in a tower, the outpost of Kansas City,
    keeps his place at a window with the serenity of a
    bronze statue on a dark night when lovers pass
    whispering.

BAND CONCERT

BAND concert public square Nebraska city. Flowing and circling dresses, summer-white dresses. Faces, flesh tints flung like sprays of cherry blossoms. And gigglers, God knows, gigglers, rivaling the pony whinnies of the Livery Stable Blues.

Cowboy rags and nigger rags. And boys driving sorrel horses hurl a cornfield laughter at the girls in dresses, summer-white dresses. Amid the cornet staccato and the tuba oompa, gigglers, God knows, gigglers daffy with life's razzle dazzle.

Slow good-night melodies and Home Sweet Home. And the snare drummer bookkeeper in a hardware store nods hello to the daughter of a railroad conductor— a giggler, God knows, a giggler—and the summer-white dresses filter fanwise out of the public square.

The crushed strawberries of ice cream soda places, the night wind in cottonwoods and willows, the lattice shadows of doorsteps and porches, these know more of the story.

THREE PIECES ON THE SMOKE OF AUTUMN

Smoke of autumn is on it all.
The streamers loosen and travel.
The red west is stopped with a gray haze.
They fill the ash trees, they wrap the oaks,
They make a long-tailed rider
In the pocket of the first, the earliest evening star.

. . .

Three muskrats swim west on the Desplaines River.

There is a sheet of red ember glow on the river; it is
    dusk; and the muskrats one by one go on patrol
    routes west.

Around each slippery padding rat, a fan of ripples; in
    the silence of dusk a faint wash of ripples, the
    padding of the rats going west, in a dark and shiver-
    ing river gold.

(A newspaper in my pocket says the Germans pierce
    the Italian line; I have letters from poets and
    sculptors in Greenwich Village; I have letters from
    an ambulance man in France and an I. W. W. man
    in Vladivostok.)

I lean on an ash and watch the lights fall, the red ember
    glow, and three muskrats swim west in a fan of
    ripples on a sheet of river gold.

. . .

Better the blue silence and the gray west,
The autumn mist on the river,
And not any hate and not any love,
And not anything at all of the keen and the deep:
Only the peace of a dog head on a barn floor,
And the new corn shoveled in bushels
And the pumpkins brought from the corn rows,
Umber lights of the dark,
Umber lanterns of the loam dark.

Here a dog head dreams.
Not any hate, not any love.
Not anything but dreams.
Brother of dusk and umber.

LOCALITIES

WAGON WHEEL GAP is a place I never saw
And Red Horse Gulch and the chutes of Cripple Creek.

Red-shirted miners picking in the sluices,
Gamblers with red neckties in the night streets,
The fly-by-night towns of Bull Frog and Skiddoo,
The night-cool limestone white of Death Valley,
The straight drop of eight hundred feet
From a shelf road in the Hasiampa Valley:
Men and places they are I never saw.

I have seen three White Horse taverns,
One in Illinois, one in Pennsylvania,
One in a timber-hid road of Wisconsin.

I bought cheese and crackers
Between sun showers in a place called White Pigeon
Nestling with a blacksmith shop, a post-office,
And a berry-crate factory, where four roads cross.

On the Pecatonica River near Freeport
I have seen boys run barefoot in the leaves
Throwing clubs at the walnut trees
In the yellow-and-gold of autumn,
And there was a brown mash dry on the inside of their
    hands.

On the Cedar Fork Creek of Knox County
I know how the fingers of late October
Loosen the hazel nuts.
I know the brown eyes of half-open hulls.
I know boys named Lindquist, Swanson, Hildebrand.
I remember their cries when the nuts were ripe.
And some are in machine shops; some are in the navy;
And some are not on payrolls anywhere.
Their mothers are through waiting for them to come
home.

CABOOSE THOUGHTS

It's going to come out all right—do you know?
The sun, the birds, the grass—they know.
They get along—and we'll get along.

Some days will be rainy and you will sit waiting
And the letter you wait for won't come,
And I will sit watching the sky tear off gray and gray
And the letter I wait for won't come.

There will be ac-ci-dents.
I know ac-ci-dents are coming.
Smash-ups, signals wrong, washouts, trestles rotten,
Red and yellow ac-ci-dents.
But somehow and somewhere the end of the run
The train gets put together again
And the caboose and the green tail lights
Fade down the right of way like a new white hope.

I never heard a mockingbird in Kentucky
Spilling its heart in the morning.

I never saw the snow on Chimborazo.
It's a high white Mexican hat, I hear.

I never had supper with Abe Lincoln.
Nor a dish of soup with Jim Hill.

But I've been around.
I know some of the boys here who can go a little.
I know girls good for a burst of speed any time.

I heard Williams and Walker
Before Walker died in the bughouse.

I knew a mandolin player
Working in a barber shop in an Indiana town,
And he thought he had a million dollars.

I knew a hotel girl in Des Moines.
She had eyes; I saw her and said to myself
The sun rises and the sun sets in her eyes.
I was her steady and her heart went pit-a-pat.
We took away the money for a prize waltz at a Brother-
    hood dance.
She had eyes; she was safe as the bridge over the Mis-
    sissippi at Burlington; I married her.

Last summer we took the cushions going west.
Pike's Peak is a big old stone, believe me.
It's fastened down; something you can count on.

It's going to come out all right—do you know?
The sun, the birds, the grass—they know.
They get along—and we'll get along.

ALIX

THE mare Alix breaks the world's trotting record one
day. I see her heels flash down the dust of an
Illinois race track on a summer afternoon. I see
the timekeepers put their heads together over stop-
watches, and call to the grand stand a split second
is clipped off the old world's record and a new
world's record fixed.

I see the mare Alix led away by men in undershirts and
streaked faces. Dripping Alix in foam of white on
the harness and shafts. And the men in undershirts
kiss her ears and rub her nose, and tie blankets on
her, and take her away to have the sweat sponged.

I see the grand stand jammed with prairie people yelling
themselves hoarse. Almost the grand stand and the
crowd of thousands are one pair of legs and one
voice standing up and yelling hurrah.

I see the driver of Alix and the owner smothered in a
fury of handshakes, a mob of caresses. I see the
wives of the driver and owner smothered in a crush
of white summer dresses and parasols.

Hours later, at sundown, gray dew creeping on the sod
and sheds, I see Alix again:
> *Dark, shining-velvet Alix,*
> *Night-sky Alix in a gray blanket,*

Led back and forth by a nigger.
Velvet and night-eyed Alix
With slim legs of steel.

And I want to rub my nose against the nose of the mare
  Alix.

POTATO BLOSSOM SONGS AND JIGS

Rum tiddy um,
tiddy um,
tiddy um tum tum.

My knees are loose-like, my feet want to sling their
selves.

I feel like tickling you under the chin—honey—and
a-asking: Why Does a Chicken Cross the Road?

When the hens are a-laying eggs, and the roosters pluck-
pluck-put-akut and you—honey—put new potatoes
and gravy on the table, and there ain't too much
rain or too little:

Say, why do I feel so gabby?
Why do I want to holler all over the place?

. . .

Do you remember I held empty hands to you
and I said all is yours
the handfuls of nothing?

. . .

I ask you for white blossoms.
I bring a concertina after sunset under the apple trees.
I bring out " The Spanish Cavalier " and " In the Gloam-
ing, O My Darling."

The orchard here is near and home-like.
The oats in the valley run a mile.
Between are the green and marching potato vines.
The lightning bugs go criss-cross carrying a zigzag of
fire: the potato bugs are asleep under their stiff

and yellow-striped wings: here romance stutters to
the western stars, " Excuse . . . me . . . ."

. . .

Old foundations of rotten wood.
An old barn done-for and out of the wormholes ten-
legged roaches shook up and scared by sunlight.
So a pickax digs a long tooth with a short memory.
Fire can not eat this rubbish till it has lain in the sun.

. . .

The story lags.
The story has no connections.
The story is nothing but a lot of banjo plinka planka
plunks.

The roan horse is young and will learn: the roan horse
buckles into harness and feels the foam on the collar
at the end of a haul: the roan horse points four
legs to the sky and rolls in the red clover: the roan
horse has a rusty jag of hair between the ears
hanging to a white star between the eyes.

. . .

In Burlington long ago
And later again in Ashtabula
I said to myself:
I wonder how far Ophelia went with Hamlet.
What else was there Shakespeare never told?
There must have been something.
If I go bugs I want to do it like Ophelia.
There was class to the way she went out of her head.

. . .

Does a famous poet eat watermelon?
Excuse me, ask me something easy.

I have seen farmhands with their faces in fried catfish
on a Monday morning.

And the Japanese, two-legged like us,
The Japanese bring slices of watermelon into pictures.
The black seeds make oval polka dots on the pink meat.

Why do I always think of niggers and buck-and-wing
dancing whenever I see watermelon?

Summer mornings on the docks I walk among bushel
peach baskets piled ten feet high.
Summer mornings I smell new wood and the river wind
along with peaches.
I listen to the steamboat whistle hong-honging, hong-
honging across the town.
And once I saw a teameo straddling a street with a hay-
rack load of melons.

. . .

Niggers play banjos because they want to.
The explanation is easy.

It is the same as why people pay fifty cents for tickets
to a policemen's masquerade ball or a grocers-and-
butchers' picnic with a fat man's foot race.
It is the same as why boys buy a nickel's worth of
peanuts and eat them and then buy another nickel's
worth.
Newsboys shooting craps in a back alley have a fugitive
understanding of the scientific principle involved.
The jockey in a yellow satin shirt and scarlet boots,
riding a sorrel pony at the county fair, has a grasp
of the theory.

It is the same as why boys go running lickety-split
    away from a school-room geography lesson
    in April when the crawfishes come out
    and the young frogs are calling
    and the pussywillows and the cat-tails
    know something about geography themselves.

        . . .

I ask you for white blossoms.
I offer you memories and people.
I offer you a fire zigzag over the green and marching
    vines.
I bring a concertina after supper under the home-like
    apple trees.
I make up songs about things to look at:
    potato blossoms in summer night mist filling the
        garden with white spots;
    a cavalryman's yellow silk handkerchief stuck in
        a flannel pocket over the left side of the shirt,
        over the ventricles of blood, over the pumps of
        the heart.

Bring a concertina after sunset under the apple trees.
Let romance stutter to the western stars, " Excuse . . .
    me . . ."

LOAM

In the loam we sleep,
In the cool moist loam,
To the lull of years that pass
And the break of stars,

From the loam, then,
The soft warm loam,
  We rise:
To shape of rose leaf,
Of face and shoulder.

  We stand, then,
  To a whiff of life,
Lifted to the silver of the sun
Over and out of the loam
  A day.

MANITOBA CHILDE ROLAND

Last night a January wind was ripping at the shingles
over our house and whistling a wolf song under the
eaves.

I sat in a leather rocker and read to a six-year-old girl
the Browning poem, *Childe Roland to the Dark
Tower Came.*

And her eyes had the haze of autumn hills and it was
beautiful to her and she could not understand.

A man is crossing a big prairie, says the poem, and
nothing happens—and he goes on and on—and it's
all lonesome and empty and nobody home.

And he goes on and on—and nothing happens—and he
comes on a horse's skull, dry bones of a dead horse—
and you know more than ever it's all lonesome and
empty and nobody home.

And the man raises a horn to his lips and blows—he
fixes a proud neck and forehead toward the empty
sky and the empty land—and blows one last wonder-
cry.

And as the shuttling automatic memory of man clicks
off its results willy-nilly and inevitable as the snick
of a mouse-trap or the trajectory of a 42-centimeter
projectile,

38

I flash to the form of a man to his hips in snow drifts
of Manitoba and Minnesota—in the sled derby run
from Winnipeg to Minneapolis.

He is beaten in the race the first day out of Winnipeg—
the lead dog is eaten by four team mates—and the
man goes on and on—running while the other racers
ride—running while the other racers sleep—

Lost in a blizzard twenty-four hours, repeating a circle
of travel hour after hour—fighting the dogs who
dig holes in the snow and whimper for sleep—
pushing on—running and walking five hundred
miles to the end of the race—almost a winner—one
toe frozen, feet blistered and frost-bitten.

And I know why a thousand young men of the Northwest meet him in the finishing miles and yell cheers
—I know why judges of the race call him a winner
and give him a special prize even though he is a
loser.

I know he kept under his shirt and around his thudding
heart amid the blizzards of five hundred miles that
one last wonder-cry of Childe Roland—and I told
the six-year-old girl all about it.

And while the January wind was ripping at the shingles
and whistling a wolf song under the eaves, her eyes
had the haze of autumn hills and it was beautiful
to her and she could not understand.

WILDERNESS

THERE is a wolf in me . . . fangs pointed for tearing
gashes . . . a red tongue for raw meat . . . and
the hot lapping of blood—I keep this wolf because
the wilderness gave it to me and the wilderness will
not let it go.

There is a fox in me . . . a silver-gray fox . . . I
sniff and guess . . . I pick things out of the wind
and air . . . I nose in the dark night and take
sleepers and eat them and hide the feathers . . . I
circle and loop and double-cross.

There is a hog in me . . . a snout and a belly . . .
a machinery for eating and grunting . . . a machinery for sleeping satisfied in the sun—I got this
too from the wilderness and the wilderness will not
let it go.

There is a fish in me . . . I know I came from salt-
blue water-gates . . . I scurried with shoals of
herring . . . I blew waterspouts with porpoises
. . . before land was . . . before the water went
down . . . before Noah . . . before the first
chapter of Genesis.

There is a baboon in me . . . clambering-clawed
. . . dog-faced . . . yawping a galoot's hunger
. . . hairy under the armpits . . . here are the

hawk-eyed hankering men . . . here are the
blond and blue-eyed women . . . here they hide
curled asleep waiting . . . ready to snarl and kill
. . . ready to sing and give milk . . . waiting—I
keep the baboon because the wilderness says so.

There is an eagle in me and a mockingbird . . . and
the eagle flies among the Rocky Mountains of my
dreams and fights among the Sierra crags of what
I want . . . and the mockingbird warbles in the
early forenoon before the dew is gone, warbles in
the underbrush of my Chattanoogas of hope, gushes
over the blue Ozark foothills of my wishes—And
I got the eagle and the mockingbird from the wilderness.

O, I got a zoo, I got a menagerie, inside my ribs, under
my bony head, under my red-valve heart—and I got
something else: it is a man-child heart, a woman-
child heart: it is a father and mother and lover:
it came from God-Knows-Where: it is going to
God-Knows-Where—For I am the keeper of the
zoo: I say yes and no: I sing and kill and work:
I am a pal of the world: I came from the wilderness.

PERSONS HALF KNOWN

CHICAGO POET

I SALUTED a nobody.
I saw him in a looking-glass.
He smiled—so did I.
He crumpled the skin on his forehead,
    frowning—so did I.
Everything I did he did.
I said, " Hello, I know you."
And I was a liar to say so.

Ah, this looking-glass man!
Liar, fool, dreamer, play-actor,
Soldier, dusty drinker of dust—
Ah! he will go with me
Down the dark stairway
When nobody else is looking,
When everybody else is gone.

He locks his elbow in mine,
I lose all—but not him.

FIRE-LOGS

NANCY HANKS dreams by the fire;
Dreams, and the logs sputter,
And the yellow tongues climb.
Red lines lick their way in flickers.
Oh, sputter, logs.
    Oh, dream, Nancy.
Time now for a beautiful child.
Time now for a tall man to come.

REPETITIONS

THEY are crying salt tears
Over the beautiful beloved body
Of Inez Milholland,
Because they are glad she lived,
Because she loved open-armed,
Throwing love for a cheap thing
Belonging to everybody—
Cheap as sunlight,
And morning air.

ADELAIDE CRAPSEY

Among the bumble-bees in red-top hay, a freckled field
of brown-eyed Susans dripping yellow leaves in
July,
     I read your heart in a book.

And your mouth of blue pansy—I know somewhere I
have seen it rain-shattered.

And I have seen a woman with her head flung between
her naked knees, and her head held there listening
to the sea, the great naked sea shouldering a load
of salt.

And the blue pansy mouth sang to the sea:
     Mother of God, I'm so little a thing,
     Let me sing longer,
     Only a little longer.

And the sea shouldered its salt in long gray combers
hauling new shapes on the beach sand.

YOUNG BULLFROGS

JIMMY WIMBLEDON listened a first week in June.
Ditches along prairie roads of Northern Illinois
Filled the arch of night with young bullfrog songs.
Infinite mathematical metronomic croaks rose and spoke,
Rose and sang, rose in a choir of puzzles.
They made his head ache with riddles of music.
They rested his head with beaten cadence.
Jimmy Wimbledon listened.

MEMOIR OF A PROUD BOY

He lived on the wings of storm.
The ashes are in Chihuahua.

Out of Ludlow and coal towns in Colorado
Sprang a vengeance of Slav miners, Italians, Scots,
Cornishmen, Yanks.
Killings ran under the spoken commands of this boy
With eighty men and rifles on a hogback mountain.

They killed swearing to remember
The shot and charred wives and children
In the burnt camp of Ludlow,
And Louis Tikas, the laughing Greek,
Plugged with a bullet, clubbed with a gun butt.

As a home war
It held the nation a week
And one or two million men stood together
And swore by the retribution of steel.

It was all accidental.
He lived flecking lint off coat lapels
Of men he talked with.
He kissed the miners' babies
And wrote a Denver paper
Of picket silhouettes on a mountain line.

He had no mother but Mother Jones
Crying from a jail window of Trinidad:
" All I want is room enough to stand
And shake my fist at the enemies of the human race."

Named by a grand jury as a murderer
He went to Chihuahua, forgot his old Scotch name,
Smoked cheroots with Pancho Villa
And wrote letters of Villa as a rock of the people.

How can I tell how Don Magregor went?

Three riders emptied lead into him.
He lay on the main street of an inland town.
A boy sat near all day throwing stones
To keep pigs away.

The Villa men buried him in a pit
With twenty Carranzistas.

There is drama in that point . . .
. . . the boy and the pigs.
Griffith would make a movie of it to fetch sobs.
Victor Herbert would have the drums whirr
In a weave with a high fiddle-string's single clamor.

"And the muchacho sat there all day throwing stones
To keep the pigs away," wrote Gibbons to the *Tribune*.

Somewhere in Chihuahua or Colorado
Is a leather bag of poems and short stories.

BILBEA

(From tablet writing, Babylonian excavations of 4th millennium B.C.)

BILBEA, I was in Babylon on Saturday night.
I saw nothing of you anywhere.
I was at the old place and the other girls were there,
but no Bilbea.

Have you gone to another house? or city?
Why don't you write?
I was sorry. I walked home half-sick.

Tell me how it goes.
Send me some kind of a letter.
And take care of yourself.

SOUTHERN PACIFIC

HUNTINGTON sleeps in a house six feet long.
Huntington dreams of railroads he built and owned.
Huntington dreams of ten thousand men saying: Yes,
   sir.

Blithery sleeps in a house six feet long.
Blithery dreams of rails and ties he laid.
Blithery dreams of saying to Huntington: Yes, sir.

Huntington,
Blithery, sleep in houses six feet long.

WASHERWOMAN

THE washerwoman is a member of the Salvation Army.
And over the tub of suds rubbing underwear clean
She sings that Jesus will wash her sins away
And the red wrongs she has done God and man
Shall be white as driven snow.
Rubbing underwear she sings of the Last Great Washday.

PORTRAIT OF A MOTOR CAR

It's a lean car . . . a long-legged dog of a car . . . a
gray-ghost eagle car.
The feet of it eat the dirt of a road . . . the wings of
it eat the hills.
Danny the driver dreams of it when he sees women in
red skirts and red sox in his sleep.
It is in Danny's life and runs in the blood of him . . .
a lean gray-ghost car.

GIRL IN A CAGE

HERE in a cage the dollars come down.
To the click of a tube the dollars tumble.
And out of a mouth the dollars run.

I finger the dollars,
Paper and silver,
Thousands a day.

Some days it's fun
        to finger the dollars.
Some days . . .
        the dollars keep on
        in a sob or a whisper:
A flame of rose in the hair,
A flame of silk at the throat.

BUFFALO BILL

Boy heart of Johnny Jones—aching to-day?
Aching, and Buffalo Bill in town?
Buffalo Bill and ponies, cowboys, Indians?

Some of us know
All about it, Johnny Jones.

Buffalo Bill is a slanting look of the eyes,
    A slanting look under a hat on a horse.
He sits on a horse and a passing look is fixed
    On Johnny Jones, you and me, barelegged,
A slanting, passing, careless look under a hat on a horse.

Go clickety-clack, O pony hoofs along the street.
Come on and slant your eyes again, O Buffalo Bill.
Give us again the ache of our boy hearts.
Fill us again with the red love of prairies, dark nights,
    lonely wagons, and the crack-crack of rifles sputter-
    ing flashes into an ambush.

SIXTEEN MONTHS

On the lips of the child Janet float changing dreams.
It is a thin spiral of blue smoke,
A morning campfire at a mountain lake.

On the lips of the child Janet,
Wisps of haze on ten miles of corn,
Young light blue calls to young light gold of morning.

CHILD MARGARET

THE child Margaret begins to write numbers on a Saturday morning, the first numbers formed under her wishing child fingers.

All the numbers come well-born, shaped in figures assertive for a frieze in a child's room.

Both 1 and 7 are straightforward, military, filled with lunge and attack, erect in shoulder-straps.

The 6 and 9 salute as dancing sisters, elder and younger, and 2 is a trapeze actor swinging to handclaps.

All the numbers are well-born, only 3 has a hump on its back and 8 is knock-kneed.

The child Margaret kisses all once and gives two kisses to 3 and 8.

(Each number is a bran-new rag doll. . . O in the wishing fingers . . . millions of rag dolls, millions and millions of new rag dolls!!)

SINGING NIGGER

YOUR bony head, Jazbo, O dock walloper,
Those grappling hooks, those wheelbarrow handlers,
The dome and the wings of you, nigger,
The red roof and the door of you,
I know where your songs came from.
I know why God listens to your, " Walk All Over God's
    Heaven."
I heard you shooting craps, " My baby's going to have
    a new dress."
I heard you in the cinders, " I'm going to live anyhow
    until I die."
I saw five of you with a can of beer on a summer night
    and I listened to the five of you harmonizing six
    ways to sing, " Way Down Yonder in the Corn-
    field."
I went away asking where I come from.

LEATHER LEGGINGS

LEATHER LEGGINGS

THEY have taken the ball of earth
    and made it a little thing.

They were held to the land and horses;
    they were held to the little seas.
They have changed and shaped and welded;
    they have broken the old tools and made
    new ones; they are ranging the white
    scarves of cloudland; they are bumping
    the sunken bells of the Carthaginians
    and Phœnicians:
                they are handling
                the strongest sea
                as a thing to be handled.

The earth was a call that mocked;
    it is belted with wires and meshed with
    steel; from Pittsburg to Vladivostok is
    an iron ride on a moving house; from
    Jerusalem to Tokyo is a reckoned span;
    and they talk at night in the storm and
    salt, the wind and the war.

They have counted the miles to the Sun
    and Canopus; they have weighed a small
    blue star that comes in the southeast
    corner of the sky on a foretold errand.

We shall search the sea again.
We shall search the stars again.
There are no bars across the way.
There is no end to the plan and the clue,
    the hunt and the thirst.
The motors are drumming, the leather leggings
    and the leather coats wait:

                Under the sea
                and out to the stars
                we go.

PRAYERS OF STEEL

Lay me on an anvil, O God.
Beat me and hammer me into a crowbar.
Let me pry loose old walls.
Let me lift and loosen old foundations.

Lay me on an anvil, O God.
Beat me and hammer me into a steel spike.
Drive me into the girders that hold a skyscraper together.
Take red-hot rivets and fasten me into the central
    girders.
Let me be the great nail holding a skyscraper through
    blue nights into white stars.

ALWAYS THE MOB

JESUS emptied the devils of one man into forty hogs and the hogs took the edge of a high rock and dropped off and down into the sea: a mob.

The sheep on the hills of Australia, blundering four-footed in the sunset mist to the dark, they go one way, they hunt one sleep, they find one pocket of grass for all.

Karnak? Pyramids? Sphinx paws tall as a coolie? Tombs kept for kings and sacred cows? A mob.

Young roast pigs and naked dancing girls of Belshazzar, the room where a thousand sat guzzling when a hand wrote: Mene, mene, tekel, upharsin? A mob.

The honeycomb of green that won the sun as the Hanging Gardens of Nineveh, flew to its shape at the hands of a mob that followed the fingers of Nebuchadnezzar: a mob of one hand and one plan.

Stones of a circle of hills at Athens, staircases of a mountain in Peru, scattered clans of marble dragons in China: each a mob on the rim of a sunrise: hammers and wagons have them now.

Locks and gates of Panama? The Union Pacific crossing deserts and tunneling mountains? The Wool-

worth on land and the *Titanic* at sea? Lighthouses
blinking a coast line from Labrador to Key West?
Pigiron bars piled on a barge whistling in a fog
off Sheboygan? A mob: hammers and wagons have
them to-morrow.

The mob? A typhoon tearing loose an island from
thousand-year moorings and bastions, shooting a
volcanic ash with a fire tongue that licks up cities
and peoples. Layers of worms eating rocks and
forming loam and valley floors for potatoes, wheat,
watermelons.

The mob? A jag of lightning, a geyser, a gravel mass
loosening. . .

The mob . . . kills or builds . . . the mob is Attila
or Ghengis Khan, the mob is Napoleon, Lincoln.

I am born in the mob—I die in the mob—the same goes
for you—I don't care who you are.

I cross the sheets of fire in No Man's land for you, my
brother—I slip a steel tooth into your throat, you my
brother—I die for you and I kill you—It is a twisted
and gnarled thing, a crimson wool:
> One more arch of stars,
> In the night of our mist,
> In the night of our tears.

JABBERERS

I RISE out of my depths with my language.
You rise out of your depths with your language.

Two tongues from the depths,
Alike only as a yellow cat and a green parrot are alike,
Fling their staccato tantalizations
Into a wildcat jabber
Over a gossamer web of unanswerables.

The second and the third silence,
Even the hundredth silence,
Is better than no silence at all
(Maybe this is a jabber too—are we at it again, you
    and I?)

I rise out of my depths with my language.
You rise out of your depths with your language.

One thing there is much of; the name men call it by is
    time; into this gulf our syllabic pronunciamentos
    empty by the way rockets of fire curve and are gone
    on the night sky; into this gulf the jabberings go
    as the shower at a scissors grinder's wheel. . . .

CARTOON

I AM making a Cartoon of a Woman.   She is the People.
   She is the Great Dirty Mother.
And Many Children hang on her Apron, crawl at her
   Feet, snuggle at her Breasts.

INTERIOR

IN the cool of the night time
The clocks pick off the points
And the mainsprings loosen.
They will need winding.
One of these days . . .
            they will need winding.

Rabelais in red boards,
Walt Whitman in green,
Hugo in ten-cent paper covers,
Here they stand on shelves
In the cool of the night time
And there is nothing . . .
To be said against them . . .
Or for them . . .
In the cool of the night time
And the clocks.

A man in pigeon-gray pyjamas.
The open window begins at his feet
And goes taller than his head.
Eight feet high is the pattern.

Moon and mist make an oblong layout.
Silver at the man's bare feet.
He swings one foot in a moon silver.
And it costs nothing.

One more day of bread and work.
One more day . . . so much rags . . .

The man barefoot in moon silver
Mutters " You " and " You "
To things hidden
In the cool of the night time,
In Rabelais, Whitman, Hugo,
In an oblong of moon mist.

Out from the window . . . prairielands.
Moon mist whitens a golf ground.
Whiter yet is a limestone quarry.
The crickets keep on chirring.

Switch engines of the Great Western
Sidetrack box cars, make up trains
For Weehawken, Oskaloosa, Saskatchewan;
The cattle, the coal, the corn, must go
In the night . . . on the prairielands.

Chuff-chuff go the pulses.
They beat in the cool of the night time.
Chuff-chuff and chuff-chuff . . .
These heartbeats travel the night a mile
And touch the moon silver at the window
And the bones of the man.
It costs nothing.

Rabelais in red boards,
Whitman in green,
Hugo in ten-cent paper covers,
Here they stand on shelves
In the cool of the night time
And the clocks.

STREET WINDOW

The pawn-shop man knows hunger,
And how far hunger has eaten the heart
Of one who comes with an old keepsake.
Here are wedding rings and baby bracelets,
Scarf pins and shoe buckles, jeweled garters,
Old-fashioned knives with inlaid handles,
Watches of old gold and silver,
Old coins worn with finger-marks.
They tell stories.

PALLADIUMS

IN the newspaper office—who are the spooks?
Who wears the mythic coat invisible?

Who pussyfoots from desk to desk
                    with a speaking forefinger?
Who gumshoes amid the copy paper
                    with a whispering thumb?

Speak softly—the sacred cows may hear.
Speak easy—the sacred cows must be fed.

CLOCKS

HERE is a face that says half-past seven the same way
whether a murder or a wedding goes on, whether
a funeral or a picnic crowd passes.

A tall one I know at the end of a hallway broods in
shadows and is watching booze eat out the insides
of the man of the house; it has seen five hopes go
in five years: one woman, one child, and three
dreams.

A little one carried in a leather box by an actress rides
with her to hotels and is under her pillow in a
sleeping-car between one-night stands.

One hoists a phiz over a railroad station; it points numbers to people a quarter-mile away who believe it
when other clocks fail.

And of course . . . there are wrist watches over the
pulses of airmen eager to go to France. . .

LEGENDS

CLOWNS DYING

FIVE circus clowns dying this year, morning newspapers
    told their lives, how each one horizontal in a last
    gesture of hands arranged by an undertaker, shook
    thousands into convulsions of laughter from behind
    rouge-red lips and powder-white face.

STEAMBOAT BILL

When the boilers of the *Robert E. Lee* exploded, a
    steamboat winner of many races on the Mississippi
    went to the bottom of the river and never again saw
    the wharves of Natchez and New Orleans.
And a legend lives on that two gamblers were blown
    toward the sky and during their journey laid bets
    on which of the two would go higher and which
    would be first to set foot on the turf of the earth
    again.

FOOT AND MOUTH PLAGUE

When the mysterious foot and mouth epidemic ravaged
    the cattle of Illinois, Mrs. Hector Smith wept bit-
    terly over the government killing forty of her soft-
    eyed Jersey cows; through the newspapers she wept
    over her loss for millions of readers in the Great
    Northwest.

75

SEVENS

The lady who has had seven lawful husbands has written
seven years for a famous newspaper telling how to
find love and keep it: seven thousand hungry girls
in the Mississippi Valley have read the instructions
seven years and found neither illicit loves nor lawful
husbands.

PROFITEER

I who saw ten strong young men die anonymously, I who
saw ten old mothers hand over their sons to the
nation anonymously, I who saw ten thousand touch
the sunlit silver finalities of undistinguished human
glory—why do I sneeze sardonically at a bronze
drinking fountain named after one who participated
in the war vicariously and bought ten farms?

PSALM OF THOSE WHO GO FORTH BEFORE DAYLIGHT

THE policeman buys shoes slow and careful; the teamster buys gloves slow and careful; they take care of their feet and hands; they live on their feet and hands.

The milkman never argues; he works alone and no one speaks to him; the city is asleep when he is on the job; he puts a bottle on six hundred porches and calls it a day's work; he climbs two hundred wooden stairways; two horses are company for him; he never argues.

The rolling-mill men and the sheet-steel men are brothers of cinders; they empty cinders out of their shoes after the day's work; they ask their wives to fix burnt holes in the knees of their trousers; their necks and ears are covered with a smut; they scour their necks and ears; they are brothers of cinders.

HORSES AND MEN IN RAIN

LET us sit by a hissing steam radiator a winter's day,
  gray wind pattering frozen raindrops on the window,
And let us talk about milk wagon drivers and grocery
  delivery boys.

Let us keep our feet in wool slippers and mix hot
  punches—and talk about mail carriers and mes-
  senger boys slipping along the icy sidewalks.
Let us write of olden, golden days and hunters of the
  Holy Grail and men called " knights " riding horses
  in the rain, in the cold frozen rain for ladies they
  loved.

A roustabout hunched on a coal wagon goes by, icicles
  drip on his hat rim, sheets of ice wrapping the hunks
  of coal, the caravanserai a gray blur in slant of rain.
Let us nudge the steam radiator with our wool slippers
  and write poems of Launcelot, the hero, and Roland,
  the hero, and all the olden golden men who rode
  horses in the rain.

QUESTIONNAIRE

Have I told any man to be a liar for my sake?

Have I sold ice to the poor in summer and coal to the poor in winter for the sake of daughters who nursed brindle bull terriers and led with a leash their dogs clothed in plaid wool jackets?

Have I given any man an earful too much of my talk— or asked any man to take a snootful of booze on my account?

Have I put wool in my own ears when men tried to tell me what was good for me? Have I been a bum listener?

Have I taken dollars from the living and the unborn while I made speeches on the retributions that shadow the heels of the dishonest?

Have I done any good under cover? Or have I always put it in the show windows and the newspapers?

NEAR KEOKUK

Thirty-two Greeks are dipping their feet in a creek.
Sloshing their bare feet in a cool flow of clear water.
All one midsummer day ten hours the Greeks
           stand in leather shoes shoveling gravel.
Now they hold their toes and ankles
           to the drift of running water.
Then they go to the bunk cars
           and eat mulligan and prune sauce,
Smoke one or two pipefuls, look at the stars,
           tell smutty stories
About men and women they have known,
           countries they have seen,
Railroads they have built—
           and then the deep sleep of children.

SLANTS AT BUFFALO, NEW YORK

A FOREFINGER of stone, dreamed by a sculptor, points to
   the sky.
It says: This way! this way!

Four lions snore in stone at the corner of the shaft.
They too are the dream of a sculptor.
They too say: This way! this way!

The street cars swing at a curve.
The middle-class passengers witness low life.
The car windows frame low life all day in pictures.

Two Italian cellar delicatessens
                  sell red and green peppers.
The Florida bananas furnish a burst of yellow.
The lettuce and the cabbage give a green.

Boys play marbles in the cinders.
The boys' hands need washing.
The boys are glad; they fight among each other.

A plank bridge leaps the Lehigh Valley railroad.
Then acres of steel rails, freight cars, smoke,
And then . . . the blue lake shore
. . . Erie with Norse blue eyes . . . and the white
   sun.

FLAT LANDS

FLAT lands on the end of town where real estate men
  are crying new subdivisions,
The sunsets pour blood and fire over you hundreds and
  hundreds of nights, flat lands—blood and fire of
  sunsets thousands of years have been pouring over
  you.
And the stars follow the sunsets. One gold star. A
  shower of blue stars. Blurs of white and gray stars.
  Vast marching processions of stars arching over you
  flat lands where frogs sob this April night.
" Lots for Sale—Easy Terms " run letters painted on a
  board—and the stars wheel onward, the frogs sob
  this April night.

LAWYER

WHEN the jury files in to deliver a verdict after weeks
of direct and cross examinations, hot clashes of
lawyers and cool decisions of the judge,
There are points of high silence—twiddling of thumbs
is at an end—bailiffs near cuspidors take fresh chews
of tobacco and wait—and the clock has a chance for
its ticking to be heard.
A lawyer for the defense clears his throat and holds
himself ready if the word is " Guilty " to enter mo-
tion for a new trial, speaking in a soft voice, speaking in a voice slightly colored with bitter wrongs
mingled with monumental patience, speaking with
mythic Atlas shoulders of many preposterous, unjust
circumstances.

THREE BALLS

Jabowsky's place is on a side street and only the rain washes the dusty three balls.

When I passed the window a month ago, there rested in proud isolation:

A family bible with hasps of brass twisted off, a wooden clock with pendulum gone,

And a porcelain crucifix with the glaze nicked where the left elbow of Jesus is represented.

I passed to-day and they were all there, resting in proud isolation, the clock and the crucifix saying no more and no less than before, and a yellow cat sleeping in a patch of sun alongside the family bible with the hasps off.

Only the rain washes the dusty three balls in front of Jabowsky's place on a side street.

CHICKS

The chick in the egg picks at the shell, cracks open one oval world, and enters another oval world.

"Cheep . . . cheep . . . cheep" is the salutation of the newcomer, the emigrant, the casual at the gates of the new world.

"Cheep . . . cheep" . . . from oval to oval, sunset to sunset, star to star.

It is at the door of this house, this teeny weeny egg-shell exit, it is here men say a riddle and jeer each other: who are you? where do you go from here?

(In the academies many books, at the circus many sacks of peanuts, at the club rooms many cigar butts.)

"Cheep . . . cheep" . . . from oval to oval, sunset to sunset, star to star.

HUMDRUM

If I had a million lives to live
    and a million deaths to die
    in a million humdrum worlds,
I'd like to change my name
    and have a new house number to go by
    each and every time I died
    and started life all over again.

I wouldn't want the same name every time
    and the same old house number always,
    dying a million deaths,
    dying one by one a million times:
    —would you?
                or you?
                        or you?

JOLIET

On the one hand the steel works.
On the other hand the penitentiary.
Sante Fé trains and Alton trains
Between smokestacks on the west
And gray walls on the east.
And Lockport down the river.

Part of the valley is God's.
And part is man's.
The river course laid out
A thousand years ago.
The canals ten years back.

The sun on two canals and one river
Makes three stripes of silver
Or copper and gold
Or shattered sunflower leaves.
    Talons of an iceberg
    Scraped out this valley.
    Claws of an avalanche loosed here.

KNUCKS

In Abraham Lincoln's city,
Where they remember his lawyer's shingle,
The place where they brought him
Wrapped in battle flags,
Wrapped in the smoke of memories
From Tallahassee to the Yukon,
The place now where the shaft of his tomb
Points white against the blue prairie dome,
In Abraham Lincoln's city . . . I saw knucks
In the window of Mister Fischman's second-hand store
On Second Street.

I went in and asked, "How much?"
"Thirty cents apiece," answered Mister Fischman.
And taking a box of new ones off a shelf
He filled anew the box in the showcase
And said incidentally, most casually
And incidentally:
"I sell a carload a month of these."

I slipped my fingers into a set of knucks,
Cast-iron knucks molded in a foundry pattern,
And there came to me a set of thoughts like these:
Mister Fischman is for Abe and the "malice to none"
    stuff,
And the street car strikers and the strike-breakers,
And the sluggers, gunmen, detectives, policemen,

Judges, utility heads, newspapers, priests, lawyers,
They are all for Abe and the " malice to none " stuff.

I started for the door.
" Maybe you want a lighter pair,"
Came Mister Fischman's voice.
I opened the door . . . and the voice again:
" You are a funny customer."

Wrapped in battle flags,
Wrapped in the smoke of memories,
This is the place they brought him,
This is Abraham Lincoln's home town.

TESTAMENT

I GIVE the undertakers permission to haul my body
to the graveyard and to lay away all, the head, the
feet, the hands, all: I know there is something left
over they can not put away.

Let the nanny goats and the billy goats of the shanty
people eat the clover over my grave   and if any yellow
hair or any blue smoke of flowers is good enough to grow
over me   let the dirty-fisted children of the shanty
people pick these flowers.

I have had my chance to live with the people who have
too much and the people who have too little and I chose
one of the two and I have told no man why.

HAUNTS

VALLEY SONG

YOUR eyes and the valley are memories.
Your eyes fire and the valley a bowl.
It was here a moonrise crept over the timberline.
It was here we turned the coffee cups upside down.
And your eyes and the moon swept the valley.

I will see you again to-morrow.
I will see you again in a million years.
I will never know your dark eyes again.
These are three ghosts I keep.
These are three sumach-red dogs I run with.

All of it wraps and knots to a riddle:
I have the moon, the timberline, and you.
All three are gone—and I keep all three.

IN TALL GRASS

BEES and a honeycomb in the dried head of a horse in
    a pasture corner—a skull in the tall grass and a
    buzz and a buzz of the yellow honey-hunters.

And I ask no better a winding sheet
                   (over the earth and under the sun.)

Let the bees go honey-hunting with yellow blur of wings
    in the dome of my head, in the rumbling, singing
    arch of my skull.

Let there be wings and yellow dust and the drone of
    dreams of honey—who loses and remembers?—who
    keeps and forgets?

In a blue sheen of moon over the bones and under the
    hanging honeycomb the bees come home and the bees
    sleep.

UPSTAIRS

I TOO have a garret of old playthings.
I have tin soldiers with broken arms upstairs.
I have a wagon and the wheels gone upstairs.
I have guns and a drum, a jumping-jack and a magic
    lantern.
And dust is on them and I never look at them upstairs.
I too have a garret of old playthings.

MONOSYLLABIC

Let me be monosyllabic to-day, O Lord.
Yesterday I loosed a snarl of words on a fool,
      on a child.
To-day, let me be monosyllabic . . . a crony of old men
      who wash sunlight in their fingers and
      enjoy slow-pacing clocks.

FILMS

I HAVE kept all, not one is thrown away, not one given
to the ragman, not one thrust in a corner with a
" P-f-f."

The red ones and the blue, the long ones in stripes, and
each of the little black and white checkered ones.

Keep them: I tell my heart: keep them another year,
another ten years: they will be wanted again.

They came once, they came easy, they came like a first
white flurry of snow in late October,

Like any sudden, presumptuous, beautiful thing, and they
were cheap at the price, cheap like snow.

Here a red one and there a long one in yellow stripes,

O there shall be no ragman have these yet a year, yet
ten years.

KREISLER

SELL me a violin, mister, of old mysterious wood.

Sell me a fiddle that has kissed dark nights on the forehead where men kiss sisters they love.

Sell me dried wood that has ached with passion clutching the knees and arms of a storm.

Sell me horsehair and rosin that has sucked at the breasts of the morning sun for milk.

Sell me something crushed in the heartsblood of pain readier than ever for one more song.

THE SEA HOLD

THE sea is large.
The sea hold on a leg of land in the Chesapeake hugs
   an early sunset and a last morning star over the
   oyster beds and the late clam boats of lonely men.
Five white houses on a half-mile strip of land . . . five
   white dice rolled from a tube.

Not so long ago . . . the sea was large . . .
And to-day the sea has lost nothing . . . it keeps all.

I am a loon about the sea.
I make so many sea songs, I cry so many sea cries, I
   forget so many sea songs and sea cries.

I am a loon about the sea.
So are five men I had a fish fry with once in a tar-paper
   shack trembling in a sand storm.
The sea knows more about them than they know them-
   selves.
They know only how the sea hugs and will not let go.

The sea is large.
The sea must know more than any of us.

GOLDWING MOTH

A GOLDWING moth is between the scissors and the ink
    bottle on the desk.
Last night it flew hundreds of circles around a glass bulb
    and a flame wire.
The wings are a soft gold; it is the gold of illuminated
    initials in manuscripts of the medieval monks.

LOIN CLOTH

Body of Jesus taken down from the cross
Carved in ivory by a lover of Christ,
It is a child's handful you are here,
The breadth of a man's finger,
And this ivory loin cloth
Speaks an interspersal in the day's work,
The carver's prayer and whim
And Christ-love.

HEMLOCK AND CEDAR

THIN sheets of blue smoke among white slabs . . .
near the shingle mill . . . winter morning.

Falling of a dry leaf might be heard . . . circular steel
tears through a log.

Slope of woodland . . . brown . . . soft . . . tinge
of blue such as pansy eyes.

Farther, field fires . . . funnel of yellow smoke . . .
spellings of other yellow in corn stubble.

Bobsled on a down-hill road . . . February snow mud
. . . horses steaming . . . Oscar the driver sings
ragtime under a spot of red seen a mile . . . the
red wool yarn of Oscar's stocking cap is seen from
the shingle mill to the ridge of hemlock and cedar.

SUMMER SHIRT SALE

THE summer shirt sale of a downtown haberdasher is glorified in a show-window slang: everybody understands the language: red dots, yellow circles, blue anchors, and dove-brown hooks, these perform explosions in color: stripes and checks fight for the possession of front lines and salients: detectives, newsies, teameoes, niggers, all stop, look, and listen: the shirt sale and the show window kick at the street with a noise joyous as a clog dancer: the ensemble is a challenge to the ghost who walks on paydays.

MEDALLION

THE brass medallion profile of your face I keep always.
It is not jingling with loose change in my pockets.
It is not stuck up in a show place on the office wall.
I carry it in a special secret pocket in the day
And it is under my pillow at night.
The brass came from a long ways off: it was up against
      hell and high water, fire and flood, before the face
      was put on it.
It is the side of a head; a woman wishes; a woman waits;
      a woman swears behind silent lips that the sea will
      bring home what is gone.

BRICKLAYER LOVE

I THOUGHT of killing myself because I am only a brick-
layer and you a woman who loves the man who runs
a drug store.

I don't care like I used to; I lay bricks straighter than
I used to and I sing slower handling the trowel
afternoons.

When the sun is in my eyes and the ladders are shaky
and the mortar boards go wrong, I think of you.

ASHURNATSIRPAL III

(From Babylonian tablet, 4,000 years Before Christ)

THREE walls around the town of Tela when I came.
They expected everything of those walls;
Nobody in the town came out to kiss my feet.

I knocked the walls down, killed three thousand soldiers,
Took away cattle and sheep, took all the loot in sight,
And burned special captives.

Some of the soldiers—I cut off hands and feet.
Others—I cut off ears and fingers.
Some—I put out the eyes.
I made a pyramid of heads.
I strung heads on trees circling the town.

When I got through with it
There wasn't much left of the town of Tela.

MAMMY HUMS

This is the song I rested with:
The right shoulder of a strong man I leaned on.
The face of the rain that drizzled on the short neck of
a canal boat.
The eyes of a child who slept while death went over and
under.
The petals of peony pink that fluttered in a shot of wind
come and gone.

This is the song I rested with:
Head, heels, and fingers rocked to the nigger mammy
humming of it, to the mile-off steamboat landing
whistle of it.

The murmurs run with bees' wings
in a late summer sun.
They go and come with white surf
slamming on a beach all day.

Get this.
And then you may sleep with a late afternoon slumber
sun.
Then you may slip your head in an elbow knowing
nothing—only sleep.
If so you sleep in the house of our song,
If so you sleep under the apple trees of our song,
Then the face of sleep must be the one face you were
looking for.

BRINGERS

Cover me over
In dusk and dust and dreams.

Cover me over
And leave me alone.

Cover me over,
You tireless, great.

Hear me and cover me,
Bringers of dusk and dust and dreams.

CRIMSON RAMBLER

Now that a crimson rambler
    begins to crawl over the house
    of our two lives—

Now that a red curve
    winds across the shingles—

Now that hands
    washed in early sunrises
    climb and spill scarlet
    on a white lattice weave—

Now that a loop of blood
    is written on our roof
    and reaching around a chimney—

How are the two lives of this house
    to keep strong hands and strong hearts?

HAUNTS

THERE are places I go when I am strong.
One is a marsh pool where I used to go
              with a long-ear hound-dog.
One is a wild crabapple tree; I was there
        a moonlight night with a girl.
The dog is gone; the girl is gone; I go to these
        places when there is no other place to go.

HAVE ME

HAVE me in the blue and the sun.
Have me on the open sea and the mountains.

When I go into the grass of the sea floor, I will go alone.
This is where I came from—the chlorine and the salt
    are blood and bones.
It is here the nostrils rush the air to the lungs. It is
    here oxygen clamors to be let in.
And here in the root grass of the sea floor I will go alone.

Love goes far. Here love ends.
Have me in the blue and the sun.

FIRE DREAMS

(Written to be read aloud, if so be, Thanksgiving Day)

I REMEMBER here by the fire,
In the flickering reds and saffrons,
They came in a ramshackle tub,
Pilgrims in tall hats,
Pilgrims of iron jaws,
Drifting by weeks on beaten seas,
And the random chapters say
They were glad and sang to God.

And so
Since the iron-jawed men sat down
And said, " Thanks, O God,"
For life and soup and a little less
Than a hobo handout to-day,
Since gray winds blew gray patterns of sleet on Plymouth
    Rock,
Since the iron-jawed men sang " Thanks, O God,"
You and I, O Child of the West,
Remember more than ever
November and the hunter's moon,
November and the yellow-spotted hills.

And so
In the name of the iron-jawed men
I will stand up and say yes till the finish is come and
    gone.
God of all broken hearts, empty hands, sleeping soldiers,
God of all star-flung beaches of night sky,
I and my love-child stand up together to-day and sing:
    " Thanks, O God."

BABY FACE

WHITE MOON comes in on a baby face.
The shafts across her bed are flimmering.

Out on the land White Moon shines,
Shines and glimmers against gnarled shadows,
All silver to slow twisted shadows
Falling across the long road that runs from the
  house.

Keep a little of your beauty
And some of your flimmering silver
For her by the window to-night
Where you come in, White Moon.

THE YEAR

I

A STORM of white petals,
Buds throwing open baby fists
Into hands of broad flowers.

II

Red roses running upward,
Clambering to the clutches of life
Soaked in crimson.

III

Rabbles of tattered leaves
Holding golden flimsy hopes
Against the tramplings
Into the pits and gullies.

IV

Hoarfrost and silence:
Only the muffling
Of winds dark and lonesome—
Great lullabies to the long sleepers.

DRUMNOTES *

Days of the dead men, Danny.
Drum for the dead, drum on your
    remembering heart.

Jaurès, a great love-heart of France,
    a slug of lead in the red valves.
Kitchener of Khartoum, tall, cold, proud,
    a shark's mouthful.
Franz Josef, the old man of forty haunted
    kingdoms, in a tomb with the Hapsburg
    fathers, moths eating a green uniform
    to tatters, worms taking all and leaving
    only bones and gold buttons, bones and
    iron crosses.
Jack London, Jim Riley, Verhaeren, riders to
    the republic of dreams.

Days of the dead, Danny.
Drum on your remembering heart.

MOONSET

Leaves of poplars pick Japanese prints against the west.
Moon sand on the canal doubles the changing pictures.
           The moon's good-by ends pictures.
The west is empty.   All else is empty.   No moon-talk
    at all now.
           Only dark listening to dark.

GARDEN WIRELESS

How many feet ran with sunlight, water, and air?

What little devils shaken of laughter, cramming their little ribs with chuckles,

Fixed this lone red tulip, a woman's mouth of passion kisses, a nun's mouth of sweet thinking, here topping a straight line of green, a pillar stem?

Who hurled this bomb of red caresses?—nodding balloon-film shooting its wireless every fraction of a second these June days:
> *Love me before I die;*
> *Love me—love me now.*

HANDFULS

Blossoms of babies
Blinking their stories
Come soft
On the dusk and the babble;
Little red gamblers,
Handfuls that slept in the dust.

Summers of rain,
Winters of drift,
Tell off the years;
And they go back
Who came soft—
Back to the sod,
To silence and dust;
Gray gamblers,
Handfuls again.

COOL TOMBS

WHEN Abraham Lincoln was shoveled into the tombs, he forgot the copperheads and the assassin . . . in the dust, in the cool tombs.

And Ulysses Grant lost all thought of con men and Wall Street, cash and collateral turned ashes . . . in the dust, in the cool tombs.

Pocahontas' body, lovely as a poplar, sweet as a red haw in November or a pawpaw in May, did she wonder? does she remember? . . . in the dust, in the cool tombs?

Take any streetful of people buying clothes and groceries, cheering a hero or throwing confetti and blowing tin horns . . . tell me if the lovers are losers . . . tell me if any get more than the lovers . . . in the dust . . . in the cool tombs.

SHENANDOAH

SHENANDOAH

In the Shenandoah Valley, one rider gray and one rider
blue, and the sun on the riders wondering.

Piled in the Shenandoah, riders blue and riders gray,
piled with shovels, one and another, dust in the
Shenandoah taking them quicker than mothers take
children done with play.

The blue nobody remembers, the gray nobody remembers,
it's all old and old nowadays in the Shenandoah.

. . .

And all is young, a butter of dandelions slung on the
turf, climbing blue flowers of the wishing woodlands
wondering: a midnight purple violet claims the sun
among old heads, among old dreams of repeating
heads of a rider blue and a rider gray in the
Shenandoah.

NEW FEET

EMPTY battlefields keep their phantoms.
Grass crawls over old gun wheels
And a nodding Canada thistle flings a purple
Into the summer's southwest wind,
Wrapping a root in the rust of a bayonet,
Reaching a blossom in rust of shrapnel.

OLD OSAWATOMIE

John Brown's body under the morning stars.
Six feet of dust under the morning stars.
And a panorama of war performs itself
Over the six-foot stage of circling armies.
Room for Gettysburg, Wilderness, Chickamauga,
On a six-foot stage of dust.

GRASS

PILE the bodies high at Austerlitz and Waterloo.
Shovel them under and let me work—
                I am the grass; I cover all.

And pile them high at Gettysburg
And pile them high at Ypres and Verdun.
Shovel them under and let me work.
Two years, ten years, and passengers ask the conductor:
                What place is this?
                Where are we now?

                I am the grass.
                Let me work.

FLANDERS

FLANDERS, the name of a place, a country of people,
Spells itself with letters, is written in books.

" Where is Flanders? " was asked one time,
Flanders known only to those who lived there
And milked cows and made cheese and spoke the home
    language.

" Where is Flanders? " was asked.
And the slang adepts shot the reply: Search me.

A few thousand people milking cows, raising radishes,
On a land of salt grass and dunes, sand-swept with a
    sea-breath on it:
This was Flanders, the unknown, the quiet,
The place where cows hunted lush cuds of green on
    lowlands,
And the raw-boned plowmen took horses with long
    shanks
Out in the dawn to the sea-breath.

Flanders sat slow-spoken amid slow-swung windmills,
Slow-circling windmill arms turning north or west,
Turning to talk to the swaggering winds, the childish
    winds,
So Flanders sat with the heart of a kitchen girl
Washing wooden bowls in the winter sun by a window.

GARGOYLE

I SAW a mouth jeering. A smile of melted red iron ran
over it. Its laugh was full of nails rattling. It
was a child's dream of a mouth.

A fist hit the mouth: knuckles of gun-metal driven by an
electric wrist and shoulder. It was a child's dream
of an arm.

The fist hit the mouth over and over, again and again.
The mouth bled melted iron, and laughed its laughter
of nails rattling.

And I saw the more the fist pounded the more the mouth
laughed. The fist is pounding and pounding, and
the mouth answering.

OLD TIMERS

I AM an ancient reluctant conscript.

On the soup wagons of Xerxes I was a cleaner of pans.

On the march of Miltiades' phalanx I had a haft and
head;
I had a bristling gleaming spear-handle.

Red-headed Cæsar picked me for a teamster.
He said, " Go to work, you Tuscan bastard,
Rome calls for a man who can drive horses."

The units of conquest led by Charles the Twelfth,
The whirling whimsical Napoleonic columns:
They saw me one of the horseshoers.

I trimmed the feet of a white horse Bonaparte swept the
night stars with.

Lincoln said, " Get into the game; your nation takes
you."
And I drove a wagon and team and I had my arm shot off
At Spottsylvania Court House.

I am an ancient reluctant conscript.

HOUSE

Two Swede families live downstairs and an Irish policeman upstairs, and an old soldier, Uncle Joe.

Two Swede boys go upstairs and see Joe. His wife is
dead, his only son is dead, and his two daughters
in Missouri and Texas don't want him around.

The boys and Uncle Joe crack walnuts with a hammer
on the bottom of a flatiron while the January wind
howls and the zero air weaves laces on the window
glass.

Joe tells the Swede boys all about Chickamauga and Chat-
tanooga, how the Union soldiers crept in rain somewhere a dark night and ran forward and killed many
Rebels, took flags, held a hill, and won a victory
told about in the histories in school.

Joe takes a piece of carpenter's chalk, draws lines on
the floor and piles stove wood to show where six
regiments were slaughtered climbing a slope.

" Here they went " and " Here they went," says Joe,
and the January wind howls and the zero air weaves
laces on the window glass.

The two Swede boys go downstairs with a big blur of
guns, men, and hills in their heads. They eat herring and potatoes and tell the family war is a wonder
and soldiers are a wonder.

One breaks out with a cry at supper: I wish we had a
war now and I could be a soldier.

JOHN ERICSSON DAY MEMORIAL, 1918

INTO the gulf and the pit of the dark night, the cold night, there is a man goes into the dark and the cold and when he comes back to his people he brings fire in his hands and they remember him in the years afterward as the fire bringer—they remember or forget—the man whose head kept singing to the want of his home, the want of his people.

For this man there is no name thought of—he has broken from jungles and the old oxen and the old wagons—circled the earth with ships—belted the earth with steel—swung with wings and a drumming motor in the high blue sky—shot his words on a wireless way through shattering sea storms:—out from the night and out from the jungles his head keeps singing—there is no road for him but on and on.

Against the sea bastions and the land bastions, against the great air pockets of stars and atoms, he points a finger, finds a release clutch, touches a button no man knew before.

The soldier with a smoking gun and a gas mask—the workshop man under the smokestacks and the blue-prints—these two are brothers of the handshake never forgotten—for these two we give the salt tears of our eyes, the salute of red roses, the flame-won scarlet of poppies.

For the soldier who gives all, for the workshop man who gives all, for these the red bar is on the flag—the red bar is the heart's-blood of the mother who gave him, the land that gave him.

The gray foam and the great wheels of war go by and take all—and the years give mist and ashes—and our feet stand at these, the memory places of the known and the unknown, and our hands give a flame-won poppy—our hands touch the red bar of a flag for the sake of those who gave—and gave all.

REMEMBERED WOMEN

For a woman's face remembered as a spot of quick light
    on the flat land of dark night,
For this memory of one mouth and a forehead they go
    on in the gray rain and the mud, they go on among
    the boots and guns.
The horizon ahead is a thousand fang flashes, it is a row
    of teeth that bite on the flanks of night, the horizon
    sings of a new kill and a big kill.
The horizon behind is a wall of dark etched with a
    memory, fixed with a woman's face—they fight on
    and on, boots in the mud and heads in the gray
    rain—for the women they hate and the women they
    love—for the women they left behind, they fight on.

OUT OF WHITE LIPS

Out of white lips a question: Shall seven million dead
ask for their blood a little land for the living wives
and children, a little land for the living brothers
and sisters?

Out of white lips:—Shall they have only air that sweeps
round the earth for breath of their nostrils and no
footing on the dirt of the earth for their battle-
drabbed, battle-soaked shoes?

Out of white lips:—Is the red in the flag the blood of
a free man on a piece of land his own or is it the
red of a sheep slit in the throat for mutton?

Out of white lips a white pain murmurs: Who shall have
land? Him who has stood ankle deep in the blood
of his comrades, in the red trenches dug in the land?

MEMOIR

PAPA JOFFRE, the shoulders of him wide as the land of France.

We look on the shoulders filling the stage of the Chicago Auditorium.

A fat mayor has spoken much English and the mud of his speech is crossed with quicksilver hisses elusive and rapid from floor and gallery.

A neat governor speaks English and the listeners ring chimes to his clear thoughts.

Joffre speaks a few words in French; this is a voice of the long firing line that runs from the salt sea dunes of Flanders to the white spear crags of the Swiss mountains.

This is the man on whose yes and no has hung the death of battalions and brigades; this man speaks of the tricolor of his country now melted in a great resolve with the starred bunting of Lincoln and Washington.

This is the hero of the Marne, massive, irreckonable;
he lets tears roll down his cheek; they trickle a wet
salt off his chin onto the blue coat.

There is a play of American hands and voices equal to
sea-breakers and a lift of white sun on a stony
beach.

A MILLION YOUNG WORKMEN, 1915

A MILLION young workmen straight and strong lay stiff
   on the grass and roads,
And the million are now under soil and their rottening
   flesh will in the years feed roots of blood-red roses.
Yes, this million of young workmen slaughtered one
   another and never saw their red hands.
And oh, it would have been a great job of killing and a
   new and beautiful thing under the sun if the million
   knew why they hacked and tore each other to death.
The kings are grinning, the kaiser and the czar—they
   are alive riding in leather-seated motor cars, and
   they have their women and roses for ease, and they
   eat fresh-poached eggs for breakfast, new butter on
   toast, sitting in tall water-tight houses reading the
   news of war.
I dreamed a million ghosts of the young workmen rose in
   their shirts all soaked in crimson . . . and yelled:
God damn the grinning kings, God damn the kaiser and
   the czar.

   Chicago, 1915.

SMOKE

I sit in a chair and read the newspapers.

Millions of men go to war, acres of them are buried,
  guns and ships broken, cities burned, villages sent
  up in smoke, and children where cows are killed
  off amid hoarse barbecues vanish like finger-rings
  of smoke in a north wind.

I sit in a chair and read the newspapers.

A TALL MAN

THE mouth of this man is a gaunt strong mouth.
The head of this man is a gaunt strong head.

The jaws of this man are bone of the Rocky Mountains,
    the Appalachians.
The eyes of this man are chlorine of two sobbing oceans,
Foam, salt, green, wind, the changing unknown.
The neck of this man is pith of buffalo prairie, old
    longing and new beckoning of corn belt or cotton
    belt,
Either a proud Sequoia trunk of the wilderness
Or huddling lumber of a sawmill waiting to be a roof.

Brother mystery to man and mob mystery,
Brother cryptic to lifted cryptic hands,
He is night and abyss, he is white sky of sun, he is the
    head of the people.
The heart of him the red drops of the people,
The wish of him the steady gray-eagle crag-hunting
    flights of the people.

Humble dust of a wheel-worn road,
Slashed sod under the iron-shining plow,
These of service in him, these and many cities, many
    borders, many wrangles between Alaska and the
    Isthmus, between the Isthmus and the Horn, and
    east and west of Omaha, and east and west of Paris,
    Berlin, Petrograd.

The blood in his right wrist and the blood in his left
wrist run with the right wrist wisdom of the many
and the left wrist wisdom of the many.
It is the many he knows, the gaunt strong hunger of
the many.

THE FOUR BROTHERS

Notes for War Songs (November, 1917)

MAKE war songs out of these;
Make chants that repeat and weave.
Make rhythms up to the ragtime chatter of the machine
    guns;
Make slow-booming psalms up to the boom of the big
    guns.
Make a marching song of swinging arms and swinging
    legs,
        Going along,
        Going along,
On the roads from San Antonio to Athens, from Seattle
    to Bagdad—
The boys and men in winding lines of khaki, the circling
    squares of bayonet points.

Cowpunchers, cornhuskers, shopmen, ready in khaki;
Ballplayers, lumberjacks, ironworkers, ready in khaki;
A million, ten million, singing, "I am ready."
This the sun looks on between two seaboards,
In the land of Lincoln, in the land of Grant and Lee.

I heard one say, "I am ready to be killed."
I heard another say, "I am ready to be killed."
O sunburned clear-eyed boys!
I stand on sidewalks and you go by with drums and guns
    and bugles,

You—and the flag!
And my heart tightens, a fist of something feels my throat
    When you go by,
You on the kaiser hunt, you and your faces saying, " I
    am ready to be killed."

They are hunting death,
Death for the one-armed mastoid kaiser.
They are after a Hohenzollern head:
There is no man-hunt of men remembered like this.

The four big brothers are out to kill.
France, Russia, Britain, America—
The four republics are sworn brothers to kill the kaiser.

Yes, this is the great man-hunt;
And the sun has never seen till now
Such a line of toothed and tusked man-killers,
In the blue of the upper sky,
In the green of the undersea,
In the red of winter dawns.
Eating to kill,
Sleeping to kill,
Asked by their mothers to kill,
Wished by four-fifths of the world to kill—
To cut the kaiser's throat,
To hack the kaiser's head,
To hang the kaiser on a high-horizon gibbet.

And is it nothing else than this?
Three times ten million men thirsting the blood
Of a half-cracked one-armed child of the German kings?
Three times ten million men asking the blood

Of a child born with his head wrong-shaped,
The blood of rotted kings in his veins?
If this were all, O God,
I would go to the far timbers
And look on the gray wolves
Tearing the throats of moose:
I would ask a wilder drunk of blood.

Look! It is four brothers in joined hands together.
      The people of bleeding France,
      The people of bleeding Russia,
      The people of Britain, the people of America—
These are the four brothers, these are the four republics.

At first I said it in anger as one who clenches his fist in
    wrath to fling his knuckles into the face of some one
    taunting;
Now I say it calmly as one who has thought it over and
    over again at night, among the mountains, by the sea-
    combers in storm.
I say now, by God, only fighters to-day will save the
    world, nothing but fighters will keep alive the names
    of those who left red prints of bleeding feet at Valley
    Forge in Christmas snow.
On the cross of Jesus, the sword of Napoleon, the skull
    of Shakespeare, the pen of Tom Jefferson, the ashes
    of Abraham Lincoln, or any sign of the red and
    running life poured out by the mothers of the world,
By the God of morning glories climbing blue the doors
    of quiet homes, by the God of tall hollyhocks laugh-
    ing glad to children in peaceful valleys, by the God
    of new mothers wishing peace to sit at windows
    nursing babies,

I swear only reckless men, ready to throw away their
   lives by hunger, deprivation, desperate clinging to
   a single purpose imperturbable and undaunted, men
   with the primitive guts of rebellion,
Only fighters gaunt with the red brand of labor's sorrow
   on their brows and labor's terrible pride in their
   blood, men with souls asking danger—only these
   will save and keep the four big brothers.

Good-night is the word, good-night to the kings, to the
   czars,
        Good-night to the kaiser.
The breakdown and the fade-away begins.
The shadow of a great broom, ready to sweep out the
   trash, is here.

One finger is raised that counts the czar,
The ghost who beckoned men who come no more—
The czar gone to the winds on God's great dustpan,
The czar a pinch of nothing,
The last of the gibbering Romanoffs.

Out and good-night—
The ghosts of the summer palaces
And the ghosts of the winter palaces!
Out and out, good-night to the kings, the czars, the
   kaisers.

Another finger will speak,
And the kaiser, the ghost who gestures a hundred million
   sleeping-waking ghosts,
The kaiser will go onto God's great dustpan—
The last of the gibbering Hohenzollerns.

Look! God pities this trash, God waits with a broom
and a dustpan,
God knows a finger will speak and count them out.

It is written in the stars;
It is spoken on the walls;
It clicks in the fire-white zigzag of the Atlantic wireless;
It mutters in the bastions of thousand-mile continents;
It sings in a whistle on the midnight winds from Walla
Walla to Mesopotamia:
Out and good-night.

The millions slow in khaki,
The millions learning *Turkey in the Straw* and *John
Brown's Body,*
The millions remembering windrows of dead at Gettys-
burg, Chickamauga, and Spottsylvania Court House,
The millions dreaming of the morning star of Appo-
mattox,
The millions easy and calm with guns and steel, planes
and prows:
There is a hammering, drumming hell to come.
The killing gangs are on the way.

God takes one year for a job.
God takes ten years or a million.
God knows when a doom is written.
God knows this job will be done and the words spoken:
Out and good-night.
The red tubes will run,
And the great price be paid,
And the homes empty,
And the wives wishing,
And the mothers wishing.

There is only one way now, only the way of the red tubes
  and the great price.

            Well . . .
Maybe the morning sun is a five-cent yellow balloon,
And the evening stars the joke of a God gone crazy.
Maybe the mothers of the world,
And the life that pours from their torsal folds—
Maybe it's all a lie sworn by liars,
And a God with a cackling laughter says:
" I, the Almighty God,
I have made all this,
I have made it for kaisers, czars, and kings."

Three times ten million men say: No.
Three times ten million men say:
            God is a God of the People.
And the God who made the world
            And fixed the morning sun,
            And flung the evening stars,
            And shaped the baby hands of life,
This is the God of the Four Brothers;
This is the God of bleeding France and bleeding Russia;
This is the God of the people of Britain and America.

The graves from the Irish Sea to the Caucasus peaks are
  ten times a million.
The stubs and stumps of arms and legs, the eyesockets
  empty, the cripples, ten times a million.
The crimson thumb-print of this anathema is on the door
  panels of a hundred million homes.
Cows gone, mothers on sick-beds, children cry a hunger
  and no milk comes in the noon-time or at night.

The death-yells of it all, the torn throats of men in
 ditches calling for water, the shadows and the hack-
 ing lungs in dugouts, the steel paws that clutch and
 squeeze a scarlet drain day by day—the storm of
 it is hell.
But look! child! the storm is blowing for a clean air.

Look! the four brothers march
And hurl their big shoulders
And swear the job shall be done.

Out of the wild finger-writing north and south, east and
 west, over the blood-crossed, blood-dusty ball of
 earth,
Out of it all a God who knows is sweeping clean,
Out of it all a God who sees and pierces through, is
 breaking and cleaning out an old thousand years, is
 making ready for a new thousand years.
The four brothers shall be five and more.

Under the chimneys of the winter time the children of
 the world shall sing new songs.
Among the rocking restless cradles the mothers of the
 world shall sing new sleepy-time songs.